THE WINE AND WISDOM SERIES No.3

NOSTALGIA

A One Act Play

GW00640700

Lynn Brittney

Published by Playstage
United Kingdom

An imprint of Write Publications Ltd

www.playsforadults.com

Designed by Kate Lowe, Greensands Graphics
Printed by Creeds Ltd, Bridport, Dorset

Note to producers about staging "Nostalgia"

This play is set in a living room on New Year's Eve. Therefore it is important to dress the set with some remnants of Christmas – perhaps a small Christmas tree, some cards, a few decorations etc. The décor is modest suburban, fairly modern.

There should be two entrances/exits – one to/from the kitchen and dining room and the other to the upstairs of the house. These can be anywhere on the stage that is convenient.

The actors represent two generations from the past, although they are not separated by many years, which should be reflected in their dress. ROY, MAURICE and EVE are in their late 60s and they represent the generation that were teenagers in the 1950s. So the men wear shirts and ties, perhaps cardigans, sensible trousers and shoes. EVE wears, perhaps, a skirt and jumper or something equally sensible. DAVID and JEAN, however, represent the generation that were teenagers in the 1960s and early 70s. JEAN should wear something a bit "ethnic" and DAVID should definitely wear designer jeans and be "rock casual". DAVID and JEAN need to give the impression that they have never abandoned their teen years but, at the same time, not look ridiculous.

DAVID and JEAN also need to emphasise their restlessness in their body language and their movements. This should contrast with the disciplined stillness, on occasions, of the other three.

The play is really about the difference in aspirations between the spoilt Baby Boomer generation and those who were children before and during WW2.

WINE AND WISDOM 3 : NOSTALGIA

CAST *(In order of appearance)*

ROY	retired man, giving in to being elderly, age late 60s
JEAN	his younger wife, impatient with Roy, age 55+
MAURICE	Roy's friend, domineering, also late 60s
EVE	Maurice's wife, overpowered by him, aged 60+
DAVID	Eve's brother, laid-back, aged 55+

2 female and 3 male parts.

The action takes place in ROY and JEAN'S living room on New Year's Eve.

WINE AND WISDOM 3
NOSTALGIA

ROY and JEAN's living room. It is 11.20 on New Year's Eve. There is a three seater sofa (facing the audience) and an easy chair, arranged at right angles and a large coffee table in the centre. There is a sideboard on the back wall and a standard lamp, which is lit. Soft jazz music is playing from a music centre stage left. There is an opening to the dining room and a door opposite to the rest of the house. The sound of voices, laughter and plates being cleared comes from the dining area.

JEAN'S VOICE OFFSTAGE	No, go in the living room. I'm just going to put this lot in the dishwasher. I'll be there in a minute....
	(DAVID enters, with a full glass of wine in his hand, followed by ROY.)
DAVID	*(calling over his shoulder)* That was a fabulous meal Jean! Thanks very much!
JEAN'S VOICE OFFSTAGE	You're welcome!
DAVID	Your wife's a great cook, Roy.
ROY	She certainly is.
DAVID	I have to thank you again for inviting me tonight.

ROY   No problem, mate. We always have Maurice and Eve round
               on New Year's Eve. Bit of a tradition now. When Eve said
               you were staying, we couldn't leave you at home on your
               own, could we?

DAVID   No, I suppose not. Still, it's a bit of an imposition.

ROY   Not at all. Messy business, divorce. I know. I've been
               through one myself.

DAVID   Well, this is my third. So I'm sort of used to it by now.

ROY   Good God! Once was enough for me. How can you afford it?

DAVID   I can't. Two…about to be three ex-wives and four children.
               It's an expensive business. That's why I'm staying with my
               sister for a while. Just 'til I sort myself out. *(DAVID sits on
               the far stage left end of the sofa. ROY sits in the chair.)*

               *(MAURICE and EVE enter. MAURICE is carrying a
               newly-opened bottle of wine and two glasses.)*

MAURICE   Have you both got glasses?

ROY   Yep.

DAVID   Sure have.

MAURICE   Right. I'll just have one myself and put the bottle in the
               middle there.

EVE   What about me, dear?

MAURICE   Sorry. Are you sure? You've had two already.

EVE   I'm not driving.

ROY   That's right. Have another glass, Evie.

EVE   Thank you, I will.

MAURICE   pours her a glass as well.

(JEAN comes in from the kitchen, wiping her hands on a tea towel. EVE sits next to DAVID and MAURICE sits next to EVE.)

JEAN   Have you got the game out?

ROY   Give people a chance, Jean. They've only just finished eating!

JEAN   Yes, but we've only got forty minutes before midnight. I thought we could play the game first.

DAVID   What game is this then?

JEAN   Nostalgia. Have you played it before?

DAVID   No.

MAURICE   What is it all about?

EVE   Oh, I'm not very good at games.

JEAN   You'll love this one. *(She goes to the sideboard and gets the box out)* I only bought it yesterday. Pour me a glass of wine Maurice.

MAURICE   Have you got a glass? Oh no, you haven't. I'll just go and get one.

JEAN   Bring those chocolates that David brought, while you're at it.

           (MAURICE exits to the dining area and JEAN puts the box on the coffee table and opens it. She arranges everything, switches off the music centre, and then sits on the floor in front of DAVID)

EVE   *(worried)* So what do you have to do, then?

JEAN   Eve, stop worrying. It's not difficult. It's all about the 1960's. You just have to answer questions on the 1960"s.

EVE   Oh, I think I can do that!

JEAN	There you are. Just made for our age group. A trip down memory lane.
DAVID	Trouble is…because of one trip too many, I may not remember the 60's.
JEAN	*(laughing)* Oh yeah? Were you an acidhead then?
DAVID	I dunno. Was I Evie?
EVE	I don't know what you were. You were a lot of trouble. I remember that. You were a bad boy.
JEAN	Ooh, do tell!
EVE	Oh,I can't remember all of it. But he was a right tearaway. Mum and Dad were beside themselves at David's antics.
DAVID	I was a bit of a shock to them, after Miss Perfect here.
ROY	You've always been a good girl, haven't you Evie?
	(MAURICE re-appears with a glass and a large box of chocolates)
MAURICE	What this about Eve?
JEAN	David was just saying that he was a shock to their Mum and Dad after Eve, who was so good.
MAURICE	I should say he was a shock. Bloody nightmare, more like.
DAVID	Oh, here we go.
MAURICE	I've never forgiven you for what you did to my Beetle.
DAVID	Jesus! That was 1965!
ROY	What did he do then?
MAURICE	He painted it in psychedelic colours while I was away on a course.
ROY	Get away!

MAURICE	I kid you not. Eve and I had just got married and we were living with her parents, while we waited for our first house to be built. I had a brand new Beetle. Straight off the assembly line. Beautiful gold finish. I go away on a weekend course with the TA and when I come back, my car looks like a hippy wagon and Eve's in tears. David here had done the deed and buggered off to a mate's house to weather the storm.
JEAN	You little devil! Why did you do it?
DAVID	Just felt like it at the time. I was only fifteen.
ROY	Why didn't you stop him, Evie?
EVE	I couldn't. I just couldn't.
MAURICE	Too soft. She's always let David walk all over her.
DAVID	*(slyly)* Part of her attraction, though, isn't it Maurice?
MAURICE	Eh? *(Shaking his head and pretending that he doesn't understand)*
JEAN	So, shall we play this game or not?
	(Everyone murmurs agreement. ROY is quite happy to play. So is DAVID. MAURICE is still seething slightly at the memory of 1965 and EVE nods but is still nervous.)
JEAN	OK. So it's quite simple. You have three dice. Oh, choose a coloured peg first, everyone. I'll be red.
DAVID	The foxy lady is red, so I'll be blue.
ROY	I'll be green.
MAURICE	I'll be yellow and Eve will be black.
DAVID	Nice of you to give her a choice.
EVE	*(nervously)* David, don't start.

(DAVID shrugs. JEAN puts all the pieces on the "Start" position on the board.)

JEAN — Right. So like I said, you have three dice. You throw the dice and the white dice tells you how many places you can move, but, you don't move until you have answered the question indicated by the numbers on all three dice.

MAURICE — What, you add the dice up?

JEAN — No. I'll show you. *(She throws the dice)* Right, the white dice says six, so if I answer the question correctly I move six places. The question is shown by the numbers on the red, white and blue dice. In that order. So, the red dice says two, the white dice says six and the blue dice says four. So Roy needs to ask me question number 264 in this book. *(She hands him the book)*

ROY — I'm with you. Hang on a minute, I need my specs.

MAURICE — So do I and so will Eve. Get them will you, dear?

(ROY gets up and retrieves his spectacles from the sideboard. EVE obediently gets two pairs of spectacles out of her bag.)

DAVID — No specs for you, Jean?

JEAN — I've got contacts.

DAVID — Quite right. Don't want to cover up those gorgeous eyes.

JEAN — Why thank you!

(MAURICE looks irritated by DAVID, but says nothing.)

ROY — Right. *(Sitting back down again)* I'm ready.

JEAN — Ok. Well that was just an example. So we'll start properly now. Maurice, you start, and Eve, you have the book,

	because you're going to have to ask him the question.
EVE	Oh, right.

(EVE looks at MAURICE nervously. MAURICE gathers up the dice, shakes them in his hand and lets them drop.)

MAURICE	Now. The white dice says five.
JEAN	So you will move five places when you have answered the question.
MAURICE	Yes. I understand that. Red is two, white is five, blue is seven. Eve, find question two five seven please.
EVE	Yes. "The twice weekly prime-time U.S. soap opera which ran from 1964 to 1968 was called...?"
MAURICE	Oh bloody hell. I never used to watch television back then.
JEAN	Too busy doing happening things, eh, Maurice?
DAVID	*(sniggering)* Yeah, right.
MAURICE	Too busy working actually. And being part of the TA. I didn't have much time for television. Give me a clue. Am I allowed a clue?
ROY	Go on. We'll let you. Only one clue mind.
EVE	Actually, it was Mum's favourite programme.
MAURICE	Oh! Yes!.....Oh, damn...what was it called? That man was in it...em...Ryan O'Neal....I know! Peyton Place!
EVE	*(relieved)* Well done, dear.
MAURICE	Right, so I move five places. Your go Eve. Pass the book to David.
EVE	*(She passes the book to DAVID and picks up the dice. She shakes them in her hand, drops them on the table but they*

roll off and drop on the floor.) Oh no!

MAURICE   Typical! No! Don't touch them! You must take them where they lie! Jean, as you're on the floor, can you see them.

JEAN   *(Getting on all fours and peering under the coffee table. DAVID leans to one side to appreciate her bum and he smiles)* Yes. I see them. Red is three, white is six and blue is one.

DAVID   *(opening the book)* "In 1965, Jean Shrimpton modelled the...what?"

EVE   *(pleased with herself)* Ooh, I know this one. It was the mini-skirt. I remember that because Maurice wouldn't let me wear one.

JEAN   You old killjoy!

MAURICE   Not at all. She was a married woman by then. It wasn't respectable. Anyway, she didn't have the legs for it.

ROY   I think Eve's got nice legs.

DAVID   *(trying to wind MAURICE up)* Andy Thomson thought she had nice legs, if I remember.

MAURICE   *(testily)* She didn't marry Andy Thomson. She married me.

JEAN   Right. David's turn. I'll have the book, thank you. Anyone want a chocolate?

    (JEAN gets up and hands the box around, while DAVID gathers up the dice from the floor and throws them.)

DAVID   Four two two.

JEAN   Hang on a minute. *(JEAN puts the chocolates down on the sideboard and reads the book standing behind DAVID)* "In the mid-60's the most trendy clothes shop at the bottom of the King's Road was called..." Oh wow! Do I remember this!

DAVID   Did you say "bottom" of the King's Road?

ROY   I wouldn't have a clue about this question. I can honestly say that I have never been to the King's Road in my life.

JEAN   You're joking!

ROY   No, I'm not.

MAURICE   Neither have I and neither has Eve.

JEAN   Good God! What about Carnaby Street?

MAURICE   No.

ROY   Oh, I think I might have gone there once. It's off Regent Street isn't it?

DAVID   Granny Takes A Trip.

JEAN   Yes! Right on! I loved that shop! I had a coat from there. It was long and black with leg of mutton sleeves. I loved that coat. So cool. I can't believe, Roy, that you have never been to the King's Road.

ROY   Why would I have wanted to go there? It was full of bloody teenagers. I was working in the City then. I didn't have time for all that fashion nonsense.

DAVID   I used to take the tube to Sloane Square and spend the whole day there. Drinking coffee, smoking a few joints and picking up chicks.

ROY   See what I mean? Teenagers behaving disgracefully.

JEAN   Mmm. It was fun being disgraceful, though, wasn't it David?

DAVID   Pure joy.

EVE   *(feeling bold)* Actually, I have been to the King's Road, Maurice.

MAURICE   *(shocked)* When?!

EVE   I used to wander along there in the seventies, after visiting Grandad in Chelsea Hospital.

JEAN   Oh. It was already fading by the seventies.

EVE   It seemed quite "hippy" to me. I used to have a coffee in a place that was all psychedelic stuff on the walls and had joss sticks burning.

MAURICE   You never told me about this.

EVE   Mm. Well I went there quite a lot. Just on my own.

DAVID   *(sarcastically, looking at MAURICE)* I wonder why?

ROY   Jean, it's your go.

JEAN   Right. Let's have the book, David. *(She takes the book, gives it to ROY and sits down on the floor again. Then she rolls the dice.)* Four one six.

ROY   Oops, glasses on again. Four one six. "In 1968, Simon and Garfunkel had a hit with…"

JEAN   Oh,oh,oh…..*(singing)* "We'd like to know a little bit about you for our files…" blah, blah, "Coo,coo,coo,choo Mrs Robinson, Heaven loves you more than you will know. Whoah, whoah, whoah"

ROY   Yes. Thank you. Don't give up the day job, will you?

               (Everyone laughs)

DAVID   Nice voice, actually.

JEAN   Thanks. I used to sing with a group.

DAVID	No! Really?
JEAN	Yeah. We were called Casey Girls. Me and two mates from school. We sang in a few gigs and then we split up.
DAVID	Where did you sing then?
JEAN	Oh the Ram Jam Club in Brixton, the Middle Earth Club in Covent Garden – a few others.
DAVID	Oh, I used to live in the Ram Jam. I saw the Stones there, before they were famous, you know.
JEAN	Yeah, I saw them there too. Never really liked the Stones.
DAVID	*(amazed)* How can you not like the Stones!
JEAN	Nah. Boys liked them. I liked more melodic stuff.
DAVID	For instance?
JEAN	Well, the Mamas and the Papas, the Beatles – you know.
DAVID	Oh yeah, hippy, drippy stuff. What a shame. And I thought we could be soul mates.
ROY	Oy, I hate to interrupt this middle-aged trip down memory lane, but it's my go now.
JEAN	Sorry, love.
ROY	You should act your age.
JEAN	Oh God! I think you act your age enough for the both of us, don't you, you miserable old bugger!
ROY	Nothing wrong in that. Our generation still understood responsibility and hard work, didn't we Maurice?
MAURICE	Absolutely.
JEAN	What do you mean "your generation"? You're only ten years older than me. Ten years doesn't count as a generation.

ROY   Ah, but where the sixties were concerned, it does. It makes
               a huge difference. When I was a teenager – well, actually, I
               wasn't a teenager, because there weren't such things when I
               was young.

DAVID   Yes there were. Teenagers were invented in the fifties.

ROY   Not in Bexleyheath they weren't. We didn't have teenagers
               in suburbia. You went to school and you were a kid. You
               left school and went to work and you were an adult. Your
               generation, was the first generation to…what were the
               words Harold MacMillan said? "You…

MAURICE   "You've never had it so good."

ROY   That's right! That's right. You never had it so good. Your
               generation had money, the like of which we'd never seen.
               When I first went out to work it took me a whole year to
               save up enough money to put a deposit on a car and then it
               took me another eight years to pay it off. When you lot
               went out to work, you all had cars just like that!

JEAN   I didn't!

ROY   I'm talking about men!

DAVID   Yeah, he's right. You had to have a set of wheels.

ROY   Thank you. I know I'm right. It was bloody annoying
               actually. There was the likes of me, in my twenties, loaded
               down with responsibility and there was the likes of him
               (pointing at DAVID) being part of the Swinging Sixties,
               with not a care in the world. Nobody normal went and
               drank coffee and got stoned in the Kings Road.

DAVID   *(pretending to be offended but actually quite amused)*
               Thank you.

ROY	*(slightly embarrassed)* Well, you know what I mean. People who weren't in their teens – who went out to work and so on. I never saw any drugs – never mind taking them. The sort of parties I went to, you just played music and talked. You know.
JEAN	*(teasing)* Oh you did go to parties, then?
ROY	*(irritated)* Course I did. I wasn't a monk.
EVE	Maurice and I used to go to some lovely parties at the TA headquarters.
ROY	I mean, I would never have dreamt of getting married in the sixties, I couldn't afford it.
EVE	*We* got married then.
ROY	Ah yes, but Maurice had a good job. He was in sales and making a fortune, selling cars to bloody teenagers.
MAURICE	True. I have to admit that I did make a good living in the sixties in the second-hand car business.
DAVID	Actually, I got married then too.
EVE	Ooh, I know! He was only nineteen. Dad went spare.
MAURICE	Yes. Nineteen, out of work and penniless. Living in a commune in Oxfordshire.
JEAN	Did you?!? I lived in a commune once.
ROY	*(amazed)* You what!? You've never mentioned this before! Why have you never mentioned this to me before?
JEAN	You never asked me.
ROY	I'm beginning to wonder what else you've kept hidden all these years.

JEAN	Are you going to play this game or are you going to stay up on the moral high ground all night?
ROY	*(aggrieved)* I'm just saying, that's all. I'd been out at work for four years when you were ten. The sixties didn't bloody swing for me.
JEAN	*(fed up with him)* I'll swing for you in a minute if you don't get on with the game!
ROY	OK. Just saying, that's all. *(He picks up the dice, hands the book to MAURICE and throws the dice)* Six one four.
MAURICE	"In 1968, the men's singles champion at Wimbledon was..?"
ROY	Now that I did have time for…
JEAN	Oh yes. Always made time for sport, dear, haven't you?
	(ROY glares at her. DAVID pours JEAN another glass of wine. She smiles at him warmly.)
ROY	Rod Laver.
MAURICE	Correct. My go again. What's the time?
EVE	Twenty to.
ROY	Have you got the champagne ready, Jean?
JEAN	Yes. All ready in the dining room.
ROY	Better bring it in here.
JEAN	I'll get it when it's time. Don't fuss.
MAURICE	*(hands the book to EVE and throws the dice.)* Four one six.
EVE	Just a minute. In 1968 Pope Paul issued an encyc…enc… *(To DAVID)* I can't say that word.
DAVID	Encyclical.

EVE	What he said. "...called Humanae Vitae, which banned what?"
MAURICE	The pill.
EVE	*(doubtful)* Well....not quite...can you expand it a bit, dear?
DAVID	*(cheekily, winking at JEAN)* She says that to him all the time.
MAURICE	Don't be smutty!
	(JEAN sniggers)
MAURICE	All sorts of contraception.
EVE	It says artificial contraception. Shall I let him have it?
JEAN	Go on. Fancy you knowing that Maurice. I wouldn't have known that.
MAURICE	I was interested in the subject.
EVE	Maurice wouldn't let me take the pill.
JEAN	What! He wouldn't let you wear a mini-skirt and he wouldn't let you take the pill! God! I see that women's liberation never got a foothold in your house then.
MAURICE	Actually, I was concerned for Jean's health and, if I may say so, I feel that I have been proved right in recent years. The dramatic rise in breast cancer, in my opinion, has a lot to do with women mucking about with their hormones.
JEAN	Well, you may be right but, still, Maurice, every woman has a right to control her own body. At least, in the sixties, we were able to throw off the Victorian attitude that women were the property of men. Except in your house, of course.
ROY	Can we get on with this game? You'll be talking about gynaecological stuff in a minute and that always makes me feel queasy.

DAVID	I think it's Eve's go.
MAURICE	*(pressing the point)* I am not, despite what you may think, a Victorian husband.
DAVID	No, he's just repressed. He can't help it.
MAURICE	*(annoyed)* Neither do I care, or have ever cared about your opinion, David. Nothing you have ever done in your life qualifies you to sit in judgment on other people.
DAVID	*(smiling)* Very true. I can't argue with that Maurice. It's just that if you weren't such a tosser, I wouldn't feel the need to keep having a pop at you.
EVE	*(horrified)* David! That's enough! Maurice has been kind enough to give you a place to stay on more than one occasion. Please show him some respect.
DAVID	*(saluting sarcastically)* Yes sir! Thank you sir!
ROY	*(sighing)* CAN we get on?
EVE	Yes. It's my go. *(She throws the dice and, this time, they stay on the table.)* Four five two.
DAVID	*(Picking up the book)* "On the 12th April 1961, the first man in space was…?"
EVE	Oh. Glenn?
MAURICE	No! Eve, why don't you listen! He said "in space" not "on the moon".
DAVID	Sorry, Eve. The answer is Yuri Gagarin.
EVE	Oh, sorry everyone.
JEAN	Don't say sorry. It's not a problem. Right, David, your go.
DAVID	Right. *(He throws the dice)* Six six six.

MAURICE	The mark of the beast. How apt.
	(DAVID just shakes his head and smiles to himself)
JEAN	"In 1967, what was the name of the song which started Flower Power?"
DAVID	*(singing)* "If you are going to San Francisco, be sure and wear some flowers in your hair. *(JEAN joins in)* "If you are going to San Francisco, you're sure to meet some groovy people there.... It's a new sensation...for a new generation..."
ROY	*(interrupting)* Oy! Hopeless hippies! We've only got ten more minutes!
	(They stop singing. DAVID winks at JEAN and she smiles.)
DAVID	Those were the days, eh? "Tune in, turn on and drop out." Or was it the other way round? "Drop out, tune in and turn on?"
JEAN	The first one, I think. My go. *(She throws the dice)* Three one six. Here's the book Roy.
ROY	Let's hope this isn't another music question. My ears have taken enough battering tonight. *(He laughs)* No. It's a question for normal people.
JEAN	Oh that means I won't be able to answer it.
ROY	"The last cricket match took place in 1962 between who?"
JEAN	And I was right. I haven't got a bloody clue.
ROY	Maurice? I bet you know this one.
MAURICE	Would it be the Gentlemen and the Players?
ROY	Well done, that man! Absolutely right. I remember that

match. Passing of an era that was. Ted Dexter was one of the last Gentlemen.

JEAN   Sorry, who were the Gentlemen and the Players?

ROY   Before you had all this "professionalism" in sport – and I say that with a sneer because I consider there's nothing professional about it anymore– you had "gentlemen" – who were amateurs and who played for the love of the sport, without payment – and the Players – who were all working class lads who played for money.

JEAN   So it was a class thing then?

ROY   Well...yes...I suppose so.

JEAN   And you're sorry that that is dead?

ROY   What?

JEAN   The upper class playing the working class at sport.

ROY   (getting heated about the subject) Ah, no. I'm not sorry about that. What I am sorry about is that sport has lost all that enthusiasm that the amateurs used to bring to it. Now it's all overpaid bastards who couldn't give a shit about sport and it's all "my people will talk to your people" and "how many products can I endorse?" palaver. If half of them were as good as they think they are, I wouldn't mind. But it's all packaging nowadays. It's all bloody hairstyles and clothes. It's not sport anymore, it's "the media". Makes me sick.

DAVID   (amazed) Wow! Such passion!

JEAN   It's about the only time he does show any, I can assure you.

ROY   You may mock! But it's your generation's fault that we lost it all.

JEAN	Again with the generation thing!
ROY	*(really getting passionate now)* All of you – a load of self-absorbed druggies, too busy "turning on" and "dropping out" to see what was valuable in society disappearing under your noses. Look what else happened in the sixties – look at what that decade destroyed! The transport system – in 1963 2,500 railway stations were closed in Britain. In 1960, they introduced traffic wardens – what an achievement that was. You had mods and rockers, Hells Angels, hippies, skinheads, Hare Krishna and just about every other unsavoury youth group knocking seven bells out of each other in the streets, taking drugs and worse – what else? Help me out here Maurice.
MAURICE	Well, you had "The Female Eunuch", women's liberation, the pill and legalized abortion.
JEAN	That was bad?
ROY	Certainly it was! Did any good ever come of it? Did it? Have women actually achieved equality?
JEAN	Well, no. I think they've just dragged themselves down to the level of men.
ROY	Exactly! As far as I can see, all women have done for themselves is to bugger about with their hormones, giving rise to God knows what illnesses, learn to drink as heavily as men, work long hours like men and their children are dragged up by an army of professional care workers.
JEAN	I think that's a bit simplistic.
ROY	*(triumphant)* Ah ha. Simplistic is it? True though. You have to admit that Women's Lib has been a disaster. Even the

women who started it all ended up going back on their word and moaning that women should stay at home and look after their kids. Look at that batty Germaine Greer. All she ever bangs on about nowadays is the menopause and HRT!

JEAN   *(sarcastically)* I had no idea you kept up with the leading lights of the Feminist Movement.

ROY   Oh that's right! Descend into sarcasm. You know I'm right.

MAURICE   Another disaster of the sixties was the whole free love movement. All that succeeded in doing was creating an epidemic of sexually transmitted diseases. Look at Aids.

DAVID   *(testily)* Aids is a disease of the 1980's, not the '60's.

MAURICE   *(pompously)* But I would beg to point out that the liberal tone set by the sixties resulted in the excesses of the next two decades.

DAVID   *(laughing)* I would beg to point out?! Maurice, you take pomposity to new heights.

ROY   *(getting annoyed)* Oy! Don't you have a go at Maurice, mate! Here he is, a successful man, about to retire. Been married to the same woman since he was twenty. Lovely house. Villa in Spain. What have you got to show for your life? Three divorces, four kids and kipping in your sister's spare room at your age!

EVE   Roy....

ROY   I'm sorry Eve. I know he's your brother but I have to speak as I find.

EVE   Yes I understand that Roy. But David isn't staying with us because he *has* to. David's a multi-millionaire. He's just staying with us while his new house is being decorated.

ROY   *(flabbergasted)* Eh?

(JEAN stares at DAVID in amazement)

MAURICE   *(bitterly)* Yes, that's right, I'm afraid, Roy. David is a multi-millionaire.

ROY   *(deflated)* Is that so?

DAVID   *(offhand)* I suppose I am worth a bit of money. I started and import, export business in the sixties...

EVE   He was only nineteen.

DAVID   I started off, actually, importing stuff from Morocco.

ROY   *(dismissively)* Drugs I suppose.

DAVID   *(irritated)* No actually. Caftans, cosmetics – stuff that the kids, at the end of the sixties, wanted to wear. Then I expanded in the seventies. That was why my first wife left me. She was disgusted at my entrepreneurial spirit. She wanted us to live on a commune and drop out totally, but I kind of liked making money. My second wife was a model. Everyone married models in the seventies. My third wife, the one I'm separating from now, just wants to do her own thing. I had set her up with a stud farm – she's mad about horses – and, in fact, she's so mad about horses that she doesn't have any interest in me. I've just bought a large apartment in London and it's being redecorated. So I decided to stay with Eve for a while. *(Pause)* That's why I can't agree with your assessment of the sixties. That decade, for me, and many others, was a decade of opportunity. We were able to build up business, catering to the new youth market. We couldn't have done it in the fifties or, probably, even, the seventies. There was just an element of freedom, magic, if you like, about the sixties. Everyone felt it.

(There is a silence)

JEAN   *(smiling to herself)* Well, I think we've done the sixties to death now, don't you?

ROY   *(sullenly)* Yes. Pack the game away. I don't feel like playing any more.

EVE   It's nearly midnight anyway.

JEAN   I'd better get the champagne. Roy, put the radio on will you?

                (JEAN exits to the dining room. ROY gets up and turns on the radio. There is some music playing. DAVID stands up.)

DAVID   I must see a man about a dog. Where's the loo?

ROY   Oh. Upstairs. Third on the left.

                (DAVID exits)

ROY   *(bitterly, to Maurice)* You might have told me he was a millionaire.

MAURICE   *(depressed)* I prefer not to think about it, Roy. Sorry.

EVE   Sorry.

ROY   I made a right idiot of myself.

EVE   Oh no ! ... you didn't...honestly... David's...well...David's not what you expect. Never has been. He was always very clever.

MAURICE   *(annoyed)* He hid it well though. When I first married Eve and we lived with her parents, I thought he was just a young tearaway. Useless, idle teenager. He used to do some

god-awful things but, all the time, that brain of his was
ticking away, looking for new opportunities to exploit.

ROY   Seems a bit daft. A millionaire having to sleep on my sofa
             tonight.

EVE   Oh David won't mind! We told him the house was a bit
             small. He's happy to go along with whatever anyone does.
             He's very easygoing.

MAURICE   *(still annoyed)* Mind like a steel trap, though, underneath
             all that laid back exterior.

ROY   Obviously.

             (Silence)

ROY   Makes you think though, doesn't it?

MAURICE   What?

ROY   About the sixties. Sometimes I think that everything I feel
             about that generation is just jealousy. I mean my youth was
             all about food rationing and living up to your parent's
             expectations. My Dad...well all the men really...who came
             back from the War...they were so damaged by it all...they
             were obsessive about wanting a quiet life. Drummed it into
             me, my Dad did, about getting a steady job, getting
             married, settling down, living until you could collect a
             decent pension. It was like all their excitement and ambition
             had been left on some French beach and they didn't have
             the will left to do anything exciting. Wasn't their fault. They
             were just bloody lucky to have survived. And we, I mean
             people our age, we had to carry the flag forward. The flag
             of stability and normality. That was what they fought for –
             so he kept telling me. They fought so we could have a

peaceful and ordered existence. So we did as we were told. We looked for the quiet life. Well, some of us did. Then along comes the next generation and, bang! Everything is turned on its head. They get the vote at eighteen, Britain starts swinging and people like me were just left bewildered. Like being the only sober person at a party. Do you know what I mean? Does this make sense to you?

MAURICE   Perfect sense. Couldn't have put it better myself.

(Silence)

EVE   *(wistfully – as an afterthought)* Still, we could have joined in, if we wanted to, couldn't we?

MAURICE   *(irritated with her)* But we *didn't* want to. Like Roy says. We were the last generation to uphold the old values.

EVE   *(pressing the point)* But we could have joined in... just a little bit.

(JEAN returns with a tray of glasses and two champagne bottles.)

JEAN   God, I had trouble opening these bottles!

EVE   I didn't hear any corks popping.

JEAN   I should hope not. Ever since I smashed an expensive light fitting in the dining room with a richocheting champagne cork, I've always covered them with tea towels before prising the corks out gently. Where's David?

EVE   Gone to the toilet.

JEAN   Thank God for that! I thought he might have left in a huff.

EVE   David wouldn't do that.

ROY   Sorry. I was a bit aggressive.

JEAN   You certainly were.

                    (DAVID returns. There is a voice from the radio)

VOICE
ON THE
RADIO   So, here we are, in the largest street party of the year. Ready
                    to hear the chimes from Big Ben that herald in the New
                    Year....

JEAN   Ooh right! Better get ready everyone! Come on, link hands!

                    *(JEAN marshals them all into a circle and they link hands.
                    JEAN positions herself in between ROY and DAVID, with
                    her back to the audience. The chimes start. They stand still,
                    while the chimes strike up to twelve. Then there is cheering
                    on the radio and loud music.)*

EVERYONE   Happy New Year!

                    *(JEAN gives ROY a peck on the lips, then she leans
                    forward and gives MAURICE a peck. ROY gives EVE a
                    peck and DAVID gives EVE a peck. Then DAVID kisses
                    JEAN, on the mouth, lingering a couple of seconds longer
                    than he should. ROY doesn't notice as he is busy shaking
                    hands with MAURICE and then he switches the radio off.)*

ROY   Come on then! Auld Lang Syne!

                    *(They all cross arms and sing Auld Lang Syne. Then JEAN
                    hands out the glasses, while ROY pours the champagne.
                    They all toast "Happy New Year", then they sit down
                    again, where they were for the board game.)*

MAURICE   I wonder what this year will hold for us all?

EVE   Well, you're going to retire finally dear.

MAURICE	Yes. I have to say that, unlike most men, I have stayed on in my job a bit longer than I should.
JEAN	Will you spend more time in Spain?
MAURICE	I expect so.
JEAN	It will be lovely.
ROY	You're lucky that you have no children still sponging off you. Even though I'm retired they still hold out the open hand.
DAVID	Oh, I didn't know you had children.
JEAN	Roy has two from his first marriage. I don't have any.
DAVID	What age are they Roy?
ROY	Er.. thirty three and thirty five.
JEAN	And still sponging off him.
ROY	Yes. It's always something. "Dad, I need a new car." "Dad I've got to pay the kids school fees". I thought when they got married and settled down they would take better care of money – but they don't.
JEAN	They're both girls, or rather, women. More champagne anyone?
	(She goes around with the bottle. Everyone accepts some more, except ROY)
ROY	Actually, I don't think I will have any more, love. I've got a bit of a headache.
JEAN	You'd better take a sleeping pill tonight, or it'll only get worse.
	(ROY nods)

ROY	I might take a cup of tea up to bed. I hope you won't mind sleeping on the sofa, David.
DAVID	No problem. Looks nice and comfortable.
MAURICE	Well, I think it's about time we said goodnight, or rather good morning. Come along Eve.
EVE	Yes dear.
MAURICE	Lovely meal, as always, Jean. We enjoy our New Year parties here, don't we Eve?
EVE	Yes we do. Maurice was saying earlier that we might get you to come out and celebrate next New Year at our villa in Spain. What do you think?
JEAN	Sounds lovely. But I can't make plans that far in advance, Eve. It does my head in.
EVE	No, well it was just a thought.
MAURICE	Come along dear.
JEAN	Do you want a hot water bottle, Eve?
EVE	Ooh yes please. If it's not too much trouble. My back's still playing me up.
JEAN	No trouble. I've got the kettle on for Roy's cup of tea anyway.
	(MAURICE and EVE exit. JEAN goes into the dining room.)
	(There is an uncomfortable silence)
DAVID	*(clearing his throat and making polite conversation)*
	Nice housing estate here. I've not been to this part of Kent before.
ROY	Well..it's nothing special. Just suburbia. It's what I'm used

to. Jean's not that keen though.

DAVID   No?

ROY   No. I think she'd like more of the bright lights... you know.
                But I'm not much of a one for big cities. She likes going on
                those City Break holidays and going to the theatre and
                such. I'm more of a snooze on the beach man, myself.

DAVID   *(giving an acceptable answer)* Right. Know what you mean.

                *(JEAN reappears, with ROY's cup of tea and a hot water
                bottle.)*

JEAN   Here you are and here's your pill.

ROY   Thanks.

JEAN   I'll just take this up to Eve and bring down David's bedding.

ROY   OK.

DAVID   Need any help?

JEAN   No. I'm fine.

                (JEAN exits. There is another uncomfortable silence.)

ROY   *(attempting to make polite conversation again)* Well, I
                wonder what this year will bring? More of the same I
                suppose. Has the current economic climate affected your
                business?

DAVID   It's been good for business really. I do a lot of trade in the
                EC now.

ROY   Ah yes. Another legacy of the sixties.

DAVID   What?

ROY   The Common Market.

DAVID   Is it?

ROY	*(goes into lecturing mode)* Well it was started in the sixties. Old De Gaulle wouldn't let us in though. On account of how much he hated us. I blame the Yanks.
DAVID	*(not really understanding)* Why?
ROY	They treated him like dirt during the Second World War. Hurt his pride. He never forgave them or us, cos we sided with them – against him.
DAVID	*(being polite)* Right. The French seemed to have overcome that now though. I have a company in Paris.
ROY	*(not really caring)* Oh yes? Doing what?
DAVID	Fashion.
ROY	*(really doesn't care)* Oh.
	(JEAN returns with some pillows and blankets and dumps them on the sofa.)
JEAN	There we are. If you just move, I'll make up the sofa.
DAVID	No, really. That's fine. I'll do it.
ROY	I think I'll make a move myself. That pill will start working in about ten minutes. Coming Jean?
JEAN	Yes love. Right. I hope you'll be OK David. Help yourself to anything in the kitchen.
DAVID	I'll be fine. Thanks. I appreciate it.
	(JEAN and ROY exit. DAVID turns on the music centre and turns down the volume. It is a Rolling Stones number and he says "Oh yes!" to himself. While he makes up the bed on the sofa, he dances and sings along with some of the lyrics. Then he sits down on the bed and looks through the book of questions about the sixties.)

DAVID *(To himself)* "In 1965, 100 soup cans were exhibited by..." - Andy Warhol. Yep. Remember that.
"During the 60's the cult hairdresser was.." Vidal Sassoon. Good mate. Had my hair cut by him. "In 1964, the first two million sellers for Manfred Mann were "Sha La La" and..."

(he sings softly) Doo wa diddy diddy dum diddy doo.

(he breaks off and says to himself) Ah, the sixties. Great times.

(He sighs and throws the book back on the table. He gets up and turns the light off. There is just the soft light from the standard lamp. He stands behind the sofa and starts to undo his shirt. The radio is playing a Mamas and Papas number. The door opens gently and JEAN is standing there, smiling. DAVID turns and smiles.)

DAVID *(softly)* Well hello foxy lady. They're playing your song.....

JEAN I just thought I'd come down and reminisce some more – now that the old folks are in bed.

DAVID Ah, yes. I rather upset them tonight, didn't I?

JEAN No. You rather upset them yesterday night. Today is a whole new day and a whole new year.

DAVID *(suggestively, picking up the dice)* Fancy another trip down memory lane?

JEAN I'm game if you are.

DAVID *(throwing the dice without taking his eyes off JEAN)* Mm. Let me see. Two seven two. When did the free love movement start?

JEAN   *(smiling slowly)* Now?

DAVID   Absolutely right. Come here and let's pretend it's the
                beginning of 1970. What do you say?

JEAN   I say "goodbye to the Swinging Sixties".

                (They kiss and the lights fade)

BLACKOUT

FURNITURE LIST

Throughout: three seater sofa; matching armchair; large coffee
                               table; sideboard; standard lamp; music centre;
                               small Christmas tree on sideboard; Christmas
                               cards; a few Christmas decorations.

PROPERTY LIST

ROY, EVE and MAURICE need reading glasses. ROY's pair is on the sideboard from the start of the play. EVE and MAURICE's are in EVE's handbag, which she brings on stage with her.

On set:	Board game "Nostalgia" is on, or in, the sideboard.
	(The components of the game are mentioned in the script).
Page 1:	DAVID : enters with a full glass of wine.
Page 2:	MAURICE: enters with a full bottle of wine and two glasses.
	EVE: enters with a handbag containing two pairs of spectacles.
Page 3:	JEAN: enters with a teatowel.
Page 4:	MAURICE: enters with a wine glass and a large box of chocolates.
Page 24:	JEAN: enters with a tray of five champagne glasses and two opened bottles of champagne.
Page 28:	JEAN: enters with a cup of tea; a "sleeping pill" and a hot water bottle.
Page 29:	JEAN: enters with two pillows and two blankets.

LIGHTING AND EFFECTS PLOT

At the start of the play there is soft background jazz music playing, the standard lamp on the stage is lit and the set lighting is normal range for an interior evening setting.

Page 3:   CUE: JEAN ...Bring those chocolates in that David brought, while you're at it...
JEAN switches music centre off.

Page 22:   CUE: JEAN ...Roy, put the radio on will you?...

ROY switches on radio. There is some music playing.

Page 24:   CUE: JEAN...You certainly were...
VOICE ON THE RADIO heralding in the New Year. The chimes start. Then there is cheering and loud music. After everyone on stage has kissed each other, ROY switches off the radio.

Page 29 :   CUE: DAVID ...Thanks. I appreciate it...
DAVID turns on the radio. It a Rolling Stones number. Volume should be kept low.

Page 30:   CUE: DAVID...Ah the sixties. Great times...
Radio music switches to a Mama and Papas number. Again, volume should be kept low.

Page 31:   CUE: JEAN...I say goodbye to the Swinging Sixties...
Music volume swells as the lights fade.